salmonpoetry

Celebrating 35 Years
of Literary Publishing

Dancing on Top
of a Broomstick

THOMAS LYDEN

With illustrations by
Ursula Klinger

salmonpoetry

Published in 2016 by
Salmon Poetry
Cliffs of Moher, County Clare, Ireland
Website: www.salmonpoetry.com
Email: info@salmonpoetry.com

ISBN 978-1-910669-57-0

COVER ARTWORK & INTERNAL ILLUSTRATIONS: Ursula Klinger

COVER DESIGN & TYPESETTING: *Siobhán Hutson*

Printed in Ireland by Sprint Print

*Salmon Poetry gratefully acknowledges the support of
The Arts Council / An Chomhairle Ealaoín*

Contents

Pulling Towards A Wild Beauty

A rushing sound sets the pace;
Wanderlust in our hearts
Makes us fawning, jostling creatures
Of the night
There's a divine creature in black
Giving us the eye
A little apparition sashaying
In the aisles
Why are we so crazy
For her?
She's still dancing as if
Alone in some world of her own
She's a long forgotten
Egyptian princess
We move towards her circle
She's there at the fulcrum
There are things that we'll never know
But tonight we're living at the hub.

POETRY LIBRARY

Smile of the Big Heart

If her big heart could only smile
It would smile at me first
Her love would be held out to me
With the gifted spirit of one
Who is truly beautiful
She's old Ireland
Standing on her own ground
She wraps her kindness
And love in generosity
And hands it to me
She comes so easily to the well
Of love and conversation
Her sensuality oozes from every pore
But she's nurturing in every sense of her being
She has kept the child's voice in her because she knows
That if she lost that she'd have nothing left to say
From the first moment I was drawn to her
I wanted her foxy hair to not resist my mouth
And knew that kissing her would be like kissing
The whole world
Her teasing laugh is like a primal scream in me
Her fire has been muted but she's
Gliding up from the turmoil
She stands before me
In ease of recognition
The ease of same souls
The ease of trust
The ease of being so deeply loved
The ease of care
The ease of tenderness
Let us now go down the sacred track
Of risk and abandonment
Let her marker fall
But let her still keep her mystery
Let me be lit up and led by her mantle.

Remembering

I can still remember
When I rode pillion
To a dance in Roundstone
And danced
With a girl who looked
Like Cathy McGowan

Someone home from England
Had a brand new suit
With drainpipe trousers
And he wore it every day
And every where

Three girls in a green Anglia
Looked like heaven
In their sailor hats and denim jeans
I remember them riding ponies
Waving at me with my
Beatle hair and yellow scarf

I joined a band with
A drumkit I couldn't play
The others plugged their
Guitars into old radios
We were going to be famous

I Want to Marry the Girl with Toilet Paper Stuck to the Sole of Her Shoe

Honest to God but one night
I spotted her coming out of
The bathroom in some local
Tourist trap
I always thought that her
Sister was much prettier
And I fancied her like hell
But just that one night
She emerged with some
Comfortable and soft pink
Paper trailing in her wake
So I took another look
And wanted it to go further
For the first time her serious mouth
Began to look pretty to me
Her frumpy clothes didn't matter any more
I started to look at her heart
And not at her skin
She'd stand beside me, but more
Importantly she'd stand before me
Beneath her too-tightly tied scarf
Her hair hung
Veronica Lake style
Just like her sister
She'd walk with me with
Old style country wisdom
Her steps imbued from the
Hobs of the safe place where she'd
Been reared.

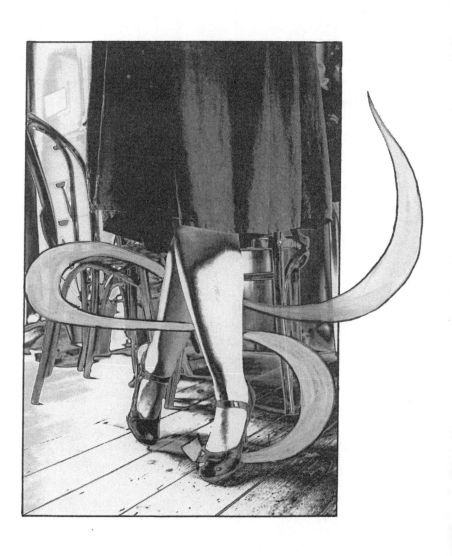

Ashamed To Be Wrong

Your voice hails away in frustration
Like a beggar hanging round till the end
Screeching through all eternity
Crippled and waiting till you descend

In a tight black dress you blow your cool
Your histrionics crucify
And you stroke your thighs in your own rhythm
And you lean on your half door with your strange loll

And you talk to all those groovy people
Walking with a sick reflex
Ashamed to be wrong
With your columns of rogues so unstable

A scorn dies and refuses
The same refrain engrained
And the hipsters are catching up with you
While your heart regales and loses

The Wall

In this room she entered
In this doorway, standing there
In her face the worry lines
Brought from time and urgency

I aged with her in this cavern
This is the universe we shared
I talked to her until midnight
She talked until a whisper

I came onto a wall
The wall was broken down
It's only now Iquestion,
It's only now I see the stones.

In A Blemished Cocoon

On the outskirts where you live
Skirmishes dance and thrash
And pain retreats down a silent street
In the enclave there's sleet and death
As shadows melt into shards
Strangeness walks on this street
In a lonely seaside town,
Where fishermen refuse to go to sea
And poets pretend to love the isolation
Where dreamers come to preen
And think that they're on to something serene
And danger wipes the smile
Across the canyon of consciousness
And uptight unhappy lumps
Shout beside a barren night
'Oh! We're creative,
We don't buy in,
But we'll sell out.'

Dancing on Top of a Broomstick

I'm tangled with you in a black car
Passing by stones and lonely scars
I'm struggling and dipped with sorrow
My wounds bathed in your wounds
Your tribulations hold me with blood ties
Prayers speak like vanity
My ordeal becomes pathetic
You drift into this wasteland
Our lovers' notes like alms
My love has become inquisitive
But I'm marble-cold
I want to sit and pray
There on your mountain
You disdain this strangeness
I float into the ether
Looking for a place to stand well on the earth
You have the fragrance of exile
Inflamed and lost in some
Tidal existence of your own.

Rhythm and Shadows

The darkness hangs about her
There are shards draining her cheeks
She came a great distance, from an ancient road
And visions creep from her aura
If you see her dance on a headland
She'll be burning like a mad dog
I have not been able to touch her
For a long time –
She bends to a rhythm of her own
And talks about celestial doom
She burns her anger in the dance,
Throwing arcs and shadows
To a wind that understands.

I'm Clashing With Her Sitting Room

I'm like something she found distasteful
And disgusting, and put in the bin,
She keeps me in an out-of-sight area of her being
I'm the serving boy,
There just to serve her.
I'd be in the scullery, and be fed on coal
If only I was drip-fed some of her attention and love
But she prefers to keep me anxious and pining
I'm the cast-out urchin
Dreaming of a loving look
From my suburban goddess
In pulled-down tracksuit bottoms
She leaves me threadbare in unrequited desire
Her clatter of activity doesn't leave any time
For doling out kindness to the likes of me
She dips in misfortune
Then blames me for ever existing,
And spoiling the look of her sitting room.

Chopstick Dave

Chopstick Dave refused to come out of his cave
Otherwise known as his aspirational country bungalow
With two ceramic horse heads on his gate pillars
Chopstick Dave somehow lost the plot or rather
He never had one in the first place
In this new Ireland we all know so well
Chopstick Dave had cut his Rasta braids
And turned his old wreck of a van into a chicken shack
He wears fewer beads around his neck
In fact he usually just wears nothing except
A simple gold chain which I see adorning
The necks of plumbers and up-and-coming gurriers
Chopstick Dave had bought the dream
Caught the ride on the pig's back
Of the Celtic tiger if that makes sense,
Well, it did to him
Chopstick Dave went along for the ride
He bought the deal as well as a new kitchen unit
Settling into his comfort zone
His bride coveting Prada
Trading in her old Lada
These two ex-bohemians had found a new drive
And I'm not talking about ground covered in tarmac
This was the roar of ascendancy
Where the only insecurity you'd feel
Was playing bridge with ladies who never seemed
To remove their headscarves
And Chopstick Dave wondered if there
Were any divorce cases where
The husband listed as one of his woes
That his wife never removed her scarf
With horse shoes emblazoned on it
And one old hairpin stuck deep in her bun

Chopstick Dave was now one of us
Cushioned on the middle of the road
Now he'd never have to read a book,
Pretend to like Radiohead,
His style from now on would be Farah slacks
With nice creases
The bride of gypsy extraction was starting
To make noises about buying him a trouser press
Imagine the prat he'd feel on Monday morning
When the refuse truck drives up to his gate just
To collect his empty trouser press box
The boys on the truck will probably think
He got some kind of a milking machine
A machine for milking your trousers, now there's a thought
If not a very painful one

    ii

What happens when the Mondeo doesn't start
What happens when the boys in the bar repeat
The same joke they told last week
What happens when teenagers sound like
They've walked off the set of 'The Hills'
What happens when golfers wear the same bloody jumper
With the same horrible insignia
What happens when the town pours sewage
Into the bay and calls it progress
What happens when the old walk on the streets
Of the town they grew up in and there's no-one there
To say hello to them
What happened to Chopstick Dave is that he saw
That the emperor had no clothes, had no wisdom
Didn't know how to stand on the ground he was destroying
Chopstick Dave and the bride had bought the dream
But the dream had no meaning any more
This is getting too serious, dear listener
But Chopstick Dave and the bride saw the light
They couldn't bear to see another poser wearing
A pink jumper around his waist

POETRY LIBRARY

Couldn't listen ever again to pretty young men
With estate agent souls pretending that they've something to say
Chopstick Dave couldn't drink out of the poison well
Of the new Ireland anymore
Let them go to hell if they haven't already
Let them drive SUVs in pointless circles
Because that would make more sense than going on about
Moving to Spain or their last holiday in Costalot
Chopstick Dave and the bride would starve themselves
for at least a week
To the point where they were hallucinating and then jack
Their chicken shack until it would take them somewhere
Beyond this Celtic disease and say goodbye to the island
Of saints and scholars, sold for a few dollars more

Style

A lampshade, a music paper
A gypsy purse that she'd taken
From her grandparents' house in Streatham
Calypso-curve, generous edging and almost
Peerless in her motion
Striding to a valley, fixed in her sureness,
I will talk to her soon
We will come back to the things
And gods we used to know

Is That An Angel I Hear Crying

Holding on to something
On this dark and narrow road
Something surely shrouds me
Savage energy scattered
So many livid angels all around
Testing avarice, testing pain
The gimpy hawkers huddle together
In a land of hurt and haunting
In the unseemly violence of the soul,
Pushing and dashing before us,
A dim wantonness all around,
Something clanging in the room
Is it good news, or an angel crying?

Please Stand Here

Please stand here
Isn't that what life is all about?
Keeping us in our place
And if your face doesn't fit, that's it.
Do you try and learn to pay bridge
Have another pretentious dinner party
Hide like a chameleon
Twist and turn until you're nowhere at all
Be seen at every dogfight
Just as long as you don't try and hog the limelight
Joining in with all the other saddoes
It's like your life is in a slot
On the average row of buying in
Don't you forget to trim your hedge
Or get your affairs in order
It's so comfortable in the shade
Trimming all your sails
You weren't born to shine
Just another shrinking violet
In the lonely walk of the insipid
A crash-course in boredom
The placid shade of convention
Inertia creeping around your door
All the whispers of failure creeping
Why is being average so acceptable?
Belonging to the cowed generation
The rules are kept and freedom's lost
The ordinary huddle together
So you put your plans on the backburner
And imagination swept aside
What is it you used to want
Was it love, joy, or money
Anyway it's now all put under wraps
And individuality is so hazardous
So you stand with the others and cackle and cant

Dressed in the clothes of the suburbanite
Is this what they call the real world
Where you don't hide your feet of clay?
Anyway we're not supposed to want so much
Or step a little out of line
We're given a small piece of the cake
And stay in our boxes
Taught never to push our luck
And sleep the sleep of the dreary
So joy has left at the station
Fate has pulled the chain on any gifts we had
Sometimes we don't know where to took
In this suburban nightmare
Is this really us or a mirage
Our solidity blanched and trembling
They'll put us in the ground
And will they praise us for not having been rebellious?

Sometimes Even the Corner Boys Go Dumb

Sometimes even the corner boys are speechless
And not able to call out their usual graceless innuendos
Or screech like animals being culled
All the dreary nobodies from small towns grow greyer
Every day from their inertia
I'm tramping out every day on this wasteland
I'm greyish-blue from trying too hard to make sense
Of the place that I come from
I'm the bard of barbs
Desperate to try and live up to my name
I'm crazy-crashing across all the nonsense
And I'm fumbling to make any sense of this life
I'm gone into the vortex and any other swirling hold
That's been carved into our own native imagination
I'm strung out on the lack of any enigmatic
Happenings in this dingy place
Crash me down with all this lassitude
Creep on all fours to be seen because
I have to face the fact that they're suffering
More and more.

The House of Correction

What if they pushed you too hard
And you fell from grace
And they take you to a strange place
Filled with shadowy figures
And you'll turn your face to the wall
It's a big hell full of visionaries, poets
And other sad cases
Where demons preach in convoluted verbiage
And card sharks will deal out the decks
But you know there will be no surprises
From tall, cloaked figures talking in the gloom
There will be psychedelic madness
Like most speedfreak gombeens
What if they keep you here forever
And throw away the key
Who'll look for your name on tombstones
What if they wipe away all your memories
And even if you could return you'd have
To live on the wrong side of town
Ensconced in this house of correction
They want to get inside your complexes
They want to make you dull and take away
Your power

A Gestalt in Black Fishnet Tights

My God, her black lycra skirt is short
But she insists it's fine
Then I see her again in a short, checked number
And her curls smelling of henna
She's the crouching feline creature draped
Around some scraggy looking hipster from out of town
She disdains the desire screeching in me
I followed her around Brown Thomas
In between the aisles
It's like she's stamped on me with all the grace
That only the truly beautiful can master
She's like a gestalt in black fishnet tights
Her walk a flame that's fired by men's passion
She's like a Welsh goddess of old
With petals scattered under her feet
As she goes down Grafton Street.

Scalded Cats in the Badlands

In streets of despair
The gangsters spit out agony
The guns spurt against innocence
Enemies flaunt tarnished gains,
Gimcrack ideologies cranking out
New blood-brothers of the back streets.
Shysters and stool-pigeons drink
The same water of destruction
Raiding an already twisted society
Sketching a punk republic
Mannequins of psychotic insecurity
Streak out into the badlands
Buying into the meat business
With lorries that cross the border
By unmarshalled roads
Daredevil hoodlums spurn convention
Using the language of the disenfranchised.
The metallic hum of their thinking
Makes the mobsters swagger with spleen
In backlots they gather deciding who's next
For the concrete overcoat.

While We're At the Bar the Poets Are Looking At the Stars for Us

So the deep thinkers all slither together
Because they're the ones who've read all the books
And think in great screeds of thought
Glowing with Jungian ideas
Reflecting with the grace
Of yet another undiscovered dead poet
Their high stools are really lofty perches
They are the furrowed brows seeking
The centre of the universe
And their tweed jackets smell
Of musty rooms where they're steeped in
The esoteric for us without us even asking
We owe them some homage for burning
So much midnight oil
They're turning forgotten pages
When we're watching our favourite soaps
They're dripping with culture
And there we are twiddling our thumbs
They're reaching for the stars
And we're heading for our local bar

Smelling Of Blood But Talking About Humility

A group of country boys
Loved shindigs and wearing dark glasses
Dreamed of dating cocktail waitresses.
Regular guys playing at being existentialists
For the evening,
Bogmen trying to work out what Marcel
Meant by creative fidelity.
Just the witless trying to work out divine acts.
They discovered Louise Lavelle and suddenly
They felt closer to God
There's a loser with his cap to the Kildare
Side talking about
The Myths Of Freedom which was written
By some Dharma Master
One of them smells of blood, but talks about humility
Next I'll hear someone talking about breaking the shell;
Or should that be the serenity of our own grief?
It's true what they say that you can dance like an idiot
In a village of goats

Fear

Fear chides like
A frightened child beneath
          The facade
In all these situations
         Of betrayal
All the isms splay their hands
The precious tones of living
          stalled
Along the arcs of power
We stumble with the struggle
Afraid of our own violence
The gate that lets in dark
Pinned against our rigidity
Like sutures in our psyche
A voice strange and blurred
Leaving scars on our souls
The phantom energy jerks
A technicolor talking stalls
In this house the blues dangles
A primitive pose strives and
          collides
Crazy dodges jaunt in the
         gorge
A cacophony screams out loud
Lathered with bad temper
The fragrance of fear
Paralyses the regulations
In this black frightened wind
Where humanity grips its ideals
In a panoramic vista of retreat
In a different time and place
Shady figures fulminate in
         frustration
The antediluvian ambition
      ambles on

In an ancient angry anthem
Slithering in shallows and starriness
Down the alley of self doubt
Scathing scoundrels steal the
                    Scene
Tomorrow's like a mirage
            On the horizon
Screaming incoherent in
                The background
Our countenances so fraught
Because the scar tissue
                Of doubt scorns
We wear a lonely furled cloak
                Drained of pride
So barren and shifty-eyed
The room of fear is fiery and crepuscular
Inside of a raiment and rainbow
The screen of vulnerability tamped
In the bum rap of ad timing
All these hurts shunt into view
Filtering into sorrow and retribution
The shards of discontentment
Stillborn in the enclave
In the mutant stages of regret
And the diminishing frowning echoes
Fear howls and destroys
In the rusty drizzle of despair
Twanging with moans of dissipation
Sparkling grotesque shapes on the anvil
The hollow testimony screams disdain
With a mouth savage and distraught
The revolt jolts with queasy impetus
The roaring of the night
Kicks like a primal notion
Drums ring out with jealousy in
The emergency beat of our hearts
Fear kisses like a conspiracy
With finality into the firmament
Where the burning exults and flames

In the cut-up trembling catchment
In the centre the rhythm shakes
On this night of a thousand angels
The desert understands our insecurity
Knowing that our anger comes
From repressed vision, our demons strike
Shuddering around the shadows
On this river of fear, like a broken mirror.

Slick O'Hara

They called you Slick O'Hara
As oily as a refinery
Now they say that this old town
Wants you back
Because all the sharpers have shown
Their hands and lost
Oh, Slick, we'll light bonfires
On your return
We'll throw all our old hatreds
In chests and drown them in the bay
We'll dress you in a white suit
And give you the finest pew in church
You can marry Mary from the creamery
She's just been pining since you went away
Just say the word now
You'll be telling us when the water
Is turned off
We all know there's no one to do it
Better than you
We'll throw that clown out of the tied cottage
And you and Mary can put your legs
Under the table
We're a dark people and we deserted you
But your pedestal is being polished up
There will be ugly heads rolling now
You're back in town
Even Jesus will shut the door on them
When they're dead

Unuch Urim and Thummim
or Light and Perfection

You try to pull towards beauty
With your guitar strumming
And your bible of contents
Screaming out for comfort
In your sacred zone
Casting lots for all kinds
Of lost causes
Kissing the belly button
Of the beast

Light the candle on the wall
Walk up and pray
At Maumeen
Walk out on a bridle path
And dream of a dead Kerry
Philosopher friend
Walk on a bog steeped
With the remnants of
Ancestors
Stone walls will beseech
You until you're able to
Lay down with your animal nature

Bragging With The Sophists

The weapon of war flutters
From calendars that point the way
Women remain greedy, from the barrel
The wise bellow and step back
Sequestering on this strange road
With all their moral and mortal reactions
The rages boom and explode
On this platform we're mesmerized,
Wily hermits retreat from the ugly
And the predictable romance of restraint
Diverting the streams of passion
Gaudy social climbers goad and go
Pushed around outside the door
Bragging with some peasant girls
Kicking the humbug out of place
In the illiterate dreams of pain
The illness of success in their bones
Hibernating from the savage elements
Fooling themselves with the darkness
Proceeding to kiss a headlock
Take the coins from the daft and
The coffee-table philosophers
Bumble in this strange and empty room
Where the vague hypocrites laud the bland
Sophism in tilted caps.

Near My Old Town

We stopped the car
By the singing bridge
And I kissed her there
I brought her down
Near to my old town
She stayed with me in that place
We walked and talked
And I lay beside her
Through all these nights
And my life became part of hers
Taking me to places of the spirit
Where I've never been before
Her hands tender on my brow
My pleasure brimming over
I'm lying in her arms
And loneliness takes a back seat

Peace and Pleasure from Connla's Well

Words spring up in me like Connla's Well
I dreamt of a crescent of beauty
That swept around me
When I didn't expect it
I couldn't have expected
Her to reach down inside of me
And pull me out of pain and dissolution
Sometimes it's like she's watching
From a long way away.
The power of her sexuality
Stuns me
It's the pull of something primal
That sacred track down into risk and abandonment
I praise all the salutary styles of her
The way she sidles up against me
And stands on my toes
Her wide-mouthed kisses stir in me
The latent passion that was doomed
By my responsibility

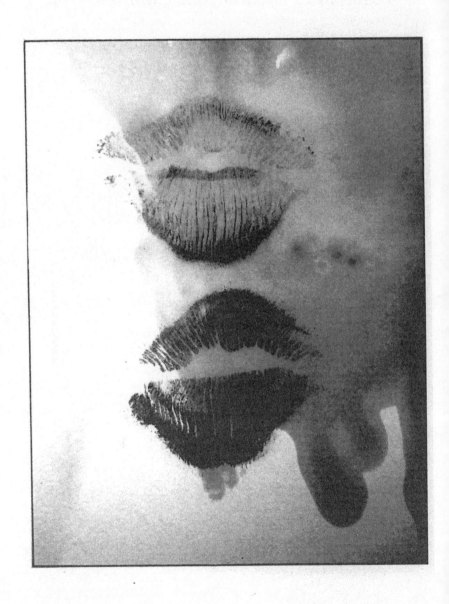

Kisses Like Vinegar

You threw a kiss at me from across the room
But somehow it was lost on me
Because I was lost in some dimension
Where women were dangerous creatures
At first their kisses taste like wine
But quickly turn into vinegar
You kiss until you bleed from disappointment
And you're hurtled into a witch's boiling brew
Denied the true nature of your being
Your balance destroyed
You shiver like mercury
In pieces across the floor.

Jumping Jasper

Jumping Jasper of the biblical name
Signs the book of lost causes
Such a dread in his head
About the town that he grew up in
Men like him with their wisdom
Honed on street corners about fifty years ago
They're now bent over the pint or two
That they can afford in the local bar
Their conversation stunted like old tars
Spitting through toothless gums
They walk limping and stooping
Looking in the market square for a nest
Or an old face that'd give them
The smallest glimpse of recognition
They're cast out on the edge of a society that's busily
Resisting knowledge and beauty
Their cosy little haven rejects the likes of them

THOMAS LYDEN was born in 1949 in the village of Faulkeeragh in Clifden, County Galway, where generations of Lydens have lived. After finishing his schooling in London and working there for a few years he came back to Clifden to help his mother on the family farm. Even while busy with the pitchfork, the pen's work would always have been on his mind. Tom Lyden was deeply aware of the magic, mystery and power of the land of Connemara and in particular of Inishbofin, the home of his mother's O'Halloran family. He was a prominent member of the arts community in Clifden. As a founding member of Baskethouse, an arts collective of local and international writers and musicians, he organized weekly readings and events in the town. His passionate interest in music, nature and his intense observation of people were major influences in his writing. His poetry has been published in various magazines and anthologies both in Ireland and abroad. In recent years Thomas moved to Dublin, but always remained connected to his Connemara roots. He passed away on December 8th, 2015.